Going Paperless

*A must-have guide for organizations
planning to go paperless and for
Enterprise Content Management
(ECM) initiatives*

AMAN BHULLAR

GOING PAPERLESS, Volume 1.0

Copyright © 2015 by AMAN BHULLAR

This book can be taken as a general guideline to plan and
implement projects for content management (ECM) and such
initiatives.

For information contact :

Aman Bhullar

amanbhullar@gmail.com

ISBN-13: 978-1539878247

ISBN-10: 1539878244

First Edition : 2015

CONTENTS

Introduction

This book is based on my experiences in implementing projects/systems that helped organization go partially or fully electronic. These initiatives are often termed as go-paperless initiatives or content management projects, or enterprise content management systems (ECM) implementations.

I must also add a disclaimer that this book is not intended to be biased towards or against any particular product or a company; it, however, is intended to share my experiences of the projects that I have been part of. I have no affiliation with any specific company or products mentioned in this book. My work can only be taken as general guideline that has worked for the projects and situations that I have dealt with. These guidelines may or may not work for the readers as every situation and project is different.

I will try to add some examples of the situations that I have been in and the ways I was able to address those. Again, those may or may not work for all the readers.

To start strategizing, let's try and understand some terms and concepts that will be useful in the implementation of ECM systems.

To get a historical perspective, let's look at the past when everything used to be paper-based. For example, to open a bank account, you had to go physically to the bank, fill a form and sign it and then hand it over to the bank. Similarly, to get a business application, or an employee asking for leave or vacation, performance evaluation, tax statements, everything was paper-based. This resulted in lots of paper that needed to be kept either for historical purposes or as part of compliance. Imagine a government department keeping the birth certificates of all the citizens within its jurisdiction over a long period of time. This has resulted in lot of paper to be stored, hence increasing the costs to store and manage paper. This also takes a heavy toll in retrieving information, when needed. It is almost as complex as finding a needle in a haystack.

With the advent of computers and technology, everyone wants the information to be readily available; plus it makes all the sense for the organizations to start storing their content in electronic format. When I refer to as content, it means documents, emails, audio files, video files, spreadsheets etc. Along with content, there is meta-data that describes the properties about the content. By definition, meta-data is a set of data that describes and gives information about other data. Confusing! Isn't it? Let's try and learn these one by one.

CONTENT MANAGEMENT - CONCEPTS

As per traditional definition: *Enterprise content management (ECM) is a formalized means of organizing and storing an organization's documents, and other content, that relate to the organization's processes. The term encompasses strategies, methods, and tools used throughout the lifecycle of the content.*

Let's take an example of resumes that a human resources (HR) department manages. In this example, let's assume, every resume is either a word document (doc) file or a pdf file. And every resume belongs to "a" candidate (for the sake of simplicity, let's assume there are 100 candidates). The doc and pdf files in this case become "content" and the candidate's name (let's break it into first-name and last-name) become "meta-data". The terms "meta-data", "attributes" and "properties" are interchangeable. So whenever I refer to any of these terms, these mean the same.

In this example, one resume contain a "file" (which is the content) and every file has some attributes – first-name and last-name are defined by the HR department (let's call them custom attributes). In addition to the custom attributes, there would be other attributes like file-name, file-size, and author of the file that can be automatically assigned by the system. So we have "a" set of custom-attributes and "a" set of system-generated-attributes. Together the content-file and the associated attributes (custom or otherwise) define the "content". This is the content that needs to be managed in "a" system.

Now these systems can either be stand-alone, or as part of a bigger enterprise system. We have seen these systems being referred to as Enterprise Content Management (ECM) systems. With the advent of Internet, lot of organizations started managing their web-based content similar to the traditional (documents) and those systems commonly started being referred to a Web Content Management (WCM) or simply Content Management Systems (CMS). Lot of Enterprise Resource Planning (ERP) systems have a component that can manage content as well.

Traditionally, ERP systems manage "structured" content. In simple terms, whatever can be organized in rows and columns (means in a database) can be termed as "structured content". Typically these databases are housed in a Relational Database Management System (RDBMS) and are driven or managed by systems like ERP systems.

In our example of resumes in an HR organization, the content is "unstructured" because along with the data (meta-data), it also has a component of actual files (pdf or doc). So in the realm of ECM systems, we are talking of managing the unstructured content within an organization.

This is an important concept to establish a baseline whenever we are trying to find a way to manage the electronic content (remember content means actual files, as well as the meta-data associated with those files). Once we find a way to house or manage the electronic content, we will find ways to convert our paper into electronic format that can be managed in an ECM system. By ECM system, I mean any component (stand-alone or within a realm of an ERP).

To summarize:

Structured information is highly defined and is intended to be processed by systems – like most of the information held in databases and acted upon by line-of-business solutions.

Unstructured information doesn't have a fully defined structure, and most likely will be read and used by humans.[1]

The most-common way to manage the electronic content is the file-system of your computer (for example, Windows Explorer in a PC, or a Finder in a Mac). Try to observe the folders, sub-folders, and files and also notice the properties (attributes or meta-data) associated with those. You can either have a centralized location to store your content or it can be in multiple locations.

Whenever we have content, it gets stored in

[1] *Source: Wikipedia*

a "repository" and there is a way to retrieve that content (for example, through a user interface – UI). There would always be a place to store the meta-data and those are typically in an RDMBS. We will not go into the details of how different systems store the content or the data.

Some systems store the files in their native formats (like pdf, doc etc), whereas others may find a way to store the files in a database (for example, as binary large objects – or blobs), and some others may convert the format of the content so that it is better manageable.

There is no right or wrong in the way these systems work; all have their own nuances. So anytime, you are dealing with ECM systems, you must be prepared to see variety of ways to store and retrieve the content.

Once you have the content in a repository, it must be "consumed"; by consumption of the content, I mean how this content is being used – either accessed by systems or individuals, or decisions to be taken, based on the status of this content etc. We will cover how to consume this content in later chapters. For now, please keep in mind that once content gets into the repository, it has to be consumed; either by humans or by other systems.

WHAT HAPPENS IF I DON'T HAVE ANY PAPER CONTENT IN MY ORGANIZATION?

ECM implementations deal with managing the content – both paper-based as well as electronic. Typically there would be a mix of paper-based content as well as content that is created electronically (such as e-mails, video files, pdf files, spreadsheets etc). There may be a need to convert paper into electronic format, or manage paper as-is.

In the subsequent chapters of this book, we

will deal with electronic content as well as look into how to convert paper (or physical content) into an electronic one, and in cases where we may still need to keep the paper (or physical records). For now, keep in mind that content has to be stored, retrieved and managed throughout its lifecycle; by lifecycle I mean various states it goes through from inception till deletion. Well, deletion maybe a strong word here; let's stick to archival (although in some cases the content may well be deleted too).

Planning & Strategy

AS WE UNDERTAKE AN ECM IMPLEMENTATION, we must address the pain points and drivers of the implementation project. Maybe the initiative is only to deal with a large volume or historical, paper-based content; or it may be to manage the existing electronic records (like invoices, HR records etc); or it may be to find a way to manage and distribute (maybe via website or through printing) the content that is there in a repository; or there are warehouses with physical tapes of an entertainment company and they want to have a way to quickly know find out the location of physical content; or to find an effective way to manage a business process of storing and retrieving books in a library. In real-life, an implementation will consist of a mix of these pain-points. First, identify what is the driver for the project/initiative. Some of the drivers can be:

- Corporate Compliance – For many organizations, such projects are driven because they need to be complying with the various regulations for storing and archiving the electronic content.
- Management Directive – Lot of organizations are driven by strategic directions of going paperless that can be part of a bigger corporate strategy.
- High Costs to Manage Paper – With increasing costs to store and inefficiencies to retrieve information

from paper-based documents, ECM initiatives are born.

- Effective Dispersal of Information – For organizations that serve public, there may be a need to effectively disperse information via websites or mobile devices. An example of this can be a government entity that wants to publish rules/codes/standards to a public-facing website.

- Business Process Automation – Your organization may want to leverage an investment in an existing platform, hence want to integrate the ECM system with other systems.

- Application Retirement – Retiring legacy systems may pave way to newer products/platforms, often resulting in some areas where ECM implementation may come handy.

- Improving Control of Information –

Organizations tend to undertake ECM projects in order to control who has the access to the content.

No matter what the project driver is, the fact is that now you have this project that you need to start working on. Let us start dissecting this initiative into smaller pieces that are more achievable and easily manageable.

A journey of a thousand miles begins with a single step.

SUCCESS CRITERIA

First and foremost is to start identifying the main driver and the biggest pain-point your project is going to address. This will help you in defining the success-criteria of the project. It is always advisable to divide the projects into smaller sub-projects so that you can start measuring and celebrating success often.

CONTENT SIZE & GROWTH

Whatever the driver is, you should know the information like how much content would need to be stored in the repository. This will help you evaluate the extent of infrastructure needed for this system.

You also want to know the rate of growth of this content. This is extremely helpful to the IT teams so that they know how much storage they need to plan to *"house"* this content. This information is also helpful in budgeting for the infrastructure – whether on premise or cloud-based implementation.

INFORMATION SECURITY

Another pertinent piece of information that needs to be known is the degree of sensitivity of this content. Do you have to store it in-house (on premise infrastructure) or can it be stored in third-party storage (for example, housed in a cloud-based system). You may want to find this out from the content owners (for example business units that manage this content).

FORMAT

What type of content are we talking about? All to be pdf files? Or you want other formats? This information will come handy when you know how various systems are managing different formats. You also want to know which formats will be covered in the immediate projects versus other formats that may be part of this ECM system later-on. An example can be that an entertainment company is investing in an ECM platform for their Accounts Payable process right now, but they would want to leverage the investment and use the same system later-on to manage the video clips (digital media) and have Digital Rights Management (DRM) features. So knowing the nature/format of the content would be helpful.

CONTENT CONSUMPTION

How this content will get consumed is a very important question that you would need answer on. The content can get into the repository and the only use-case may be to search and retrieve (maybe based on attributes or full-text searched). In that case, we are looking for a simple(r) implementation where we need to identify the attributes and ways to search the content. There may be other ways to consume this content. Does it need to be routed in a workflow and decisions to be taken or not? Does it have life-cycle (for example; draft, review, approve, archive). What do the users (or systems) do with this content, depending on various stages it resides in?

What happens to the content once it is in a repository? Do you want to retain this content as per retention policies or do you need to store it as an official record? Who (the users or group of users etc) has what type of access (delete, read, view etc) on this content at what time (status – draft, approved etc)?

You need to ensure that the appropriate people have the appropriate access at the appropriate content at the appropriate time.

Whenever you discuss the content-consumption, you can think of how the content is provided to the users. Some systems create "renditions" so that the users only access renditions and not the actual content files. An example can be a word document stored in a repository; however, a pdf rendition gets created upon "approval" and is sent to the user.

When you are discussing the search and retrieval, you may want to find out if the users want to search the text within the content files.

We call it full-text search; generally an ECM system will have its own search-engine to perform this function. Depending on the system you wish to choose, the search can be either attribute-based, or full-text, or both.

CONTENT ORGANIZATION

Content organization is another important aspect. Some systems allow the creation of folders and sub-folders for organization of the content. This is visually appealing, as well as, keeps the content organized in a repository. There are other systems that may take the approach of creating a bucket of files and rely solely on their powerful search mechanism to find the relevant content. Organizing the content in folders and hierarchy of folders is referred to as a "browsing" approach, which can be cumbersome, but lot of users may prefer it because that is the way they are used to.

Keeping a bucket approach may be easy to

implement, solely relying on the search-engines. It can, however, be slightly confusing for some users because they may not know where their file is stored: resulting in some resistance from the users.

There is no right or wrong in either of the approaches. I have found that a good balance of organizing the content into folders and sub-folders and also relying on the search has yielded positive results: the users can visually see how their content is organized (no overdoing this please!) and they can search for their content either using attribute search or using full-text search.

INGESTION

In simple terms, this means how the content will get into the repository. Are we adding a scanning piece to the puzzle, or we are looking at users creating the content electronically (for example, invoices etc).

Invariably, all the projects will cover this aspect of content management. No matter if users are going to be scanning going forward, or scanning the historical paper-files, or just working with the electronic files to start-with; this aspect of the project will go hand-in-hand with the identified attributes.

You need to know which attributes are required versus optional. There are always going to be some system-generated attributes. So you need to start identifying the attributes and see how can you leverage those in your process.

In the realm of the discussion in this book, we will focus solely on scanning the paper. Apart from paper, there can be other stuff that may need to be scanned; maybe there are microfilms in an organization, or an old film in an entertainment company that wants to digitize that film into electronic files (those may need specialized scanners). For the ease of simplicity, we will stick to paper being scanned using the paper-scanners.

Talking to the end-users, by learning their day-to-day functions, search-criteria and talking to a functional analyst can help you find out answers to these questions. The idea is that you need to know all the details of this aspect in your project.

In lot of projects where I have been involved in, there has been a component of bulk-ingestion. That simply means that papers are scanned, or electronic content is already there in a file-system and we had to write utilities to ingest that content into a repository. Addressing this can also help you to find out if there is a migration from an existing system or not. Invariably, there would be either content sitting somewhere in an organization that needs to be moved into the repository.

If you are only implementing a day-forward process, then the ingestion would simply mean the ways to get the content via a user interface (UI). This UI can either be a thick-client or a thin-client or a combination of these; just like the repository can either be in a cloud or on premise. The decision to adopt a specific UI would rest a lot on the way how users work with the content.

In my experience, there is no single UI that can serve *all* the purposes for *all* the users. You may want to think of rolling out a combination of multiple UI. For example, there may be mobile users who just need to approve the content in its lifecycle; versus some other users who need to edit the content on daily basis; versus there may be a public-facing portal where the content from within the repository needs to be published. Depending on how users are going to interact, you should select the appropriate UI for appropriate users.

Plus it does not make financial sense to be investing in a feature-rich UI license whereas some users (actually most) might just need a simple(r) interface that can either be custom-built or can be purchased cheap(er). There are lots of options to choose from. You just need to do your due diligence. If you are thinking of these aspects and approaching your projects holistically, you would find the *biggest bang for your buck*.

There can be some specific use-cases where you may have to take input from a stream of text, convert those into documents (maybe pdf) and then store them in the repository. This is typically in cases where the organizations receive the data either from another system, or from external parties. This can fit well in case of an Electronic Data Interchange (EDI) scenario.

CONTENT
BEHAVIOR/AUTOMATION

Now that we have thought of having a repository (either central or not), we can now think of how to have users work with the content. When I say *work* on the content here, I don't mean by just the ways for editing or deleting the content. The content (or files) invariably would need to be routed amongst various parts of the organization. These processes can either be a simple workflow, or it can be a complex process of integrating with other systems. I recall, in one of the projects that I did, we had interfaces with the post-office, along with various ERP systems, along with interfaces to get feedback from the users (human interfaces).

Whenever the content needs to be routed from the repository, we can define it as business process management (BPM). The BPM, these days is an inherent function of the ECM systems. Whenever you start an ECM project, you need to know if you would need BPM capabilities or not. Often, you can start nimble with some basic Document Management (often called library services), and then add BPM or automation at a later time.

Scanning, Storing and Distribution

SCANNING is the process of digitizing whatever you have on paper (or on a physical object – like microfilms etc). Just think of taking a picture of a piece of paper so that it becomes an electronic file. The exact format of the electronic files depends on what do you want to do with the electronic content. Often, you would see the tiff format to be prevalent when it comes to scanned images. Some systems handle tiff very well, others would prefer to have them converted to text-searchable pdf files. We will not get into what is the best format to handle scans in the scope of this book. The instructions in this book can give you general guidelines on things to consider in an ECM implementation.

Along with scanning (the process of using the scanner to take a picture and produce the electronic file), you would need to consider the *indexing*. By indexing, I mean, assigning the meta-data to the image (that a scanner generates). In short, you need to holistically think of a scanning/imaging strategy whenever you have to deal with paper.

SCANNING/IMAGING STRATEGY

Scanning strategy is generally beyond just making a decision to buy a (or few) scanner(s). You need to consider whether you would have centralized scanning or distributed scanning. Which staff resources would be doing purely scanning versus indexing? Always ask yourself if it is a high volume scanning set-up where you may have to dedicate specific staff members to only do the scanning part and not worry about indexing. There can be scenarios where you want the scanning staff to perform indexing operations. A mailroom that receives hundreds of thousands of letters every day may warrant dedicated scanning staff. There is whole process of preparing the paper for scanning (often called as document preparation). Do not ignore the time and effort would it take your scanning staff for document preparation. Looking at the type of paper that needs to be scanned, its volume, its quality (shrivelled, folded, torn paper is often a reality in high volume scenarios) will help you determine the scanning needs.

This is an area where there is, typically, a scope to improve the process. If you don't have scanning facility and you are new to this type of a setup, you would notice that you can add lot of efficiencies in your process. Talk to the experts to identify if there is a scope to improve the business process.

When you think of scanning, you have to think of people (users) that will need to interface with scanners and paper. It is fairly common to have browser-based scanning as almost all of the systems these days provide that capability. In my experience, a combination of thick-clients and browser-based clients has been the most beneficial. Do your homework and you would know which one is best for your organization.

You can easily find seamless connection (integrations) between the scanner (hardware), scanning software and the repository. After some research, you can find the best solution for your needs. Some people also prefer direct scanning from a multi-function device (MFD) into the repository.

When you think of ingestion/scanning, it is pertinent to look at other ingestion mechanisms that have to be considered.

We may have an insurance company that receives lot of faxes (maybe sent to a centralized fax-server); a simple integration can be to route these incoming faxes into a network location that gets watched for any incoming traffic and the faxes (presumably already electronic) are routed for indexing.

Similar to a centralized fax server, we can also see use-cases where emails can be sent (maybe with attachments) to a centralized email queue. That queue can also be watched by a piece of software for ingestion.

Whatever the case is, you have to take a look at all of the ingestion points.

Now let's come to "indexing". Indexing is a term that is loosely used to indicate applying meta-data to the electronic files. I have heard terms like "coding", "validation", or "indexing" to depict this function. The idea being that you have an electronic file and that needs to be *indexed* (for the meta-data) to indicate information (maybe like a case number, invoice number, invoice amount, document ID etc).

The question is "how do we get this information (index or meta-data)?"

We can either rely on what is called as an OCR (optical character recognition) process. It simply means that the machine (*software*) reads the image and gets some meaningful information in a human language.

As per the traditional definition, *Optical character recognition (optical character reader, OCR) is the mechanical or electronic conversion of images of typed, handwritten or printed text into machine-encoded text, whether from a scanned document, a photo of a document, a scene-photo (for example the text on signs and billboards in a landscape photo) or from subtitle text superimposed on an image (for example from a television broadcast). It is widely used as a form of information entry from printed paper data records, whether passport documents, invoices, bank statements, computerized receipts, business cards, mail, printouts of static-data, or any suitable documentation. It is a common method of digitizing printed texts so that they can be electronically edited, searched, stored more compactly, displayed on-line, and used in machine processes such as cognitive computing, machine translation, (extracted) text-to-speech, key data and text mining. OCR is a field of research in pattern recognition, artificial intelligence and computer vision.*

Early versions needed to be trained with images of each character, and worked on one font at a time. Advanced systems capable of producing a high degree of recognition accuracy for most fonts are now common, and with support for a variety of digital image file format inputs. Some systems are capable of reproducing formatted output that closely approximates the original page including images, columns, and other non-textual components.[2]

OCR systems have evolved greatly and you will hear terms like ICR (intelligent character recognition) or OMR (optical magnetic recognition) etc. Basic idea is to get the information from a picture (*of a paper*) and convert it into data (that can either be read by

[2] *Source: Wikipedia*

humans or by machines). You will find variety of systems that either specializes in this area, or you may have to rely on such capabilities of the scanning system.

You do, however, have to make a decision on the accuracy of the results. The accuracy of the results will come from the type of system that you are investing in and also on the quality of the original source *(paper in this case).*

To give an example, if a human has hand-written "8" on a piece of paper and it looks like a "B" even to a human eye, it is likely that the machine will read it as a "B": unless you have configured it in such a way that it should only look for numeric characters. Also, there is, invariably, a degree of accuracy in these systems. Based on the type of information you are trying to capture, you may want to look for the degree of accuracy of OCR. Let's call it "accuracy threshold".

Typically, your business users will tell you how much of accuracy threshold they are willing to accept in a system. For example, if the information is not that sensitive in your business process, you may be okay to accept "B" for an "8" in our example earlier. If your content is more sensitive, you may want to increase the accuracy-threshold so that the system can help make decisions to route it to a human (for example) to make a determination of the data coming out from the OCR system.

So OCR can contribute to the indexing function in a scanning scenario. If a machine can read the information from an image, this information can be used for indexing (applying the meta-data) to the content. Applying meta-data can either be in specific "attributes" that co-exist with the content, or it can simply reside as a full-text OCR'd information that will eventually help the users "search" for the required content. We will cover the search/retrieval mechanisms in the later sections of this book.

Now that we have an image, and the associated OCR information, the indexing can either be done automatically or this information be routed for users to do the indexing. Often times, we find that indexing users simply verify (or correct) the information that the machine has given them. You do not want 100% of human indexing, or a 100% of machine indexing (validation). In my experience, a mix of the two is generally which gives the best results. Again, you would need to look at the use-case scenario and the type of information and the accuracy of the scanning/OCR systems.

Often, I observe the check-scanning and indexing that takes place in an ATM machine. I would say that all the checks that I have personally deposited have gone through with the correct information. Now it is up to the banks if they want to route these checks (images and meta-data) to humans, or they want to accept whatever the machine has given them. It all depends on your business scenario. The key here is that OCR systems read the information from paper and make that information available for humans or systems to act on.

I am sure all the product manufacturers have these bells and whistles in their products. You should certainly try to explore all the possibilities that suit your use-case.

In scanning and indexing scenario, there may be some quality Assurance (QA) queues where already-indexed documents can be passed over. It is generally done to keep a check of the indexing quality in an organization.

Almost all the products these days have something called machine-learning for automatic classification. That is generally an advanced function that comes with scanning systems. In simple terms, it means that the software will learn on-the-fly about the images that it goes through and keep improving its classification.

Use of bar-codes is also a common way for classification and indexing. Try and understand how different products handle those.

Coming back to OCR, it is not just for content that is being ingested via scanning process. There might be images in your repository that need to be OCR'd. In few projects that I have handled, we wrote some utilities that will go through the content in the repository and as soon as they encounter the content that needs to be OCR'd, it passes that content to an OCR engine and place the OCR'd files (generally pdf) back into the repository. That way, the content that is OCR'd is available for full-text searches.

The basic idea of going through the exercise of looking at scanning strategy is to ensure that you have thought-through the use-cases and see how individual products will handle those.

TAXONOMY

After we have found way to get the content into the repository, we should now think of how will be organized in the repository. Some people may call it taxonomy. Taxonomy is much more than simply organizing. By definition: *Taxonomy (from Greek "taxis" meaning arrangement or division and "nomos" meaning law) is the science of classification according to a pre-determined system with the resulting catalog used to provide a conceptual framework for discussion, analysis, or information retrieval.*[3]

[3] *Source: Wikipedia*

Taxonomy is different than meta-data in a way that taxonomy helps you to organize the content into *hierarchical relationships*. It helps it easier for the users to search or browse to the appropriate content when they aren't specifically sure of what they are looking for. It generally has a specific use with a logical hierarchy and is generally in lines with the corporate standards within an organization.

Some people prefer the use of folders and sub-folders, whereas, others may find it redundant to have folders within a content management system. It is individual preference, but it also depends on the capabilities of a particular system that is being implemented. It is nothing but a logical way to organize content that is not only visually appealing, but also helps users navigate (or browse) through the repository.

In an ideal scenario, if a document is full-text indexed, and is tagged with the appropriate attributes; and last, but not the least, if you have an advanced/modern search-engine, you should be able to find the content within one search; no matter whether it is organized in folders or not. We all use search-engines on daily basis. So whenever you are thinking of having a corporate repository, take into account how the search will be used by the users. How easy or cumbersome is it to have users go to that particular file that they are interested in.

An example of using folders can be to store a personnel file in an HR department. There can be sub-folders for commendations, awards, disciplinary record, vacation record, performance record and so on. And the top folder can be based on an employee ID or a name. The idea is that if an HR staff member is looking for an employee, he/she searches only for the employee

ID/name and then the entire package is available and then from there, the user can then "browse" to other sub-folders that belong to that employee. This can be an example of using search to reach the top folder and then browsing to the sub-folders and files underneath. A mix of the approaches is what is going to be beneficial in the adoption of the system by users. Similarly, there can be examples of creating top level folders for things like insurance policy, investigation case, clients, vendors etc.

Having folders and sub-folders will also help *organize* the security of the content. You may have a scenario where certain users have "read-only" access to certain sub-folders, whereas IT may not have any access; or IT may just want to know if a file exists or not. Most of the products these days have a robust security and multiple tiers of access to the content. Getting a good understanding of which users need to work on which content will help you create your security mechanism in your system. Remember: *You need to ensure that the appropriate people have the appropriate access at the appropriate content at the appropriate time.*

When you think of security, you should also try and discuss the encryption options available. I am sure your security guys will thank you for considering that in your project. There are various encryptions available these days. You can look at encryption being offered for calls from the users to the repository *(and back)*. I am sure you can easily find products these days that will ensure encryption of the traffic going back and forth.

In addition to the traffic-encryption, you can also look at encryption of content at-rest. After carefully looking at all the options available and based on how sensitive the content (or data) is, you can finalize the best solution for your encryption needs. The point is, if you have security and encryption that is of importance, you should look for options available: for content transmission as well as for content at-rest.

ATTRIBUES (META-DATA)

Now let's come to the attributes; more attributes, easier is it to search the content *(based on those attribute values)*. I will be questioned by some people here: if the content is full-text indexed, then what s the need of attributes? My answer is that full-text search is very capable these days, but it will, invariably, bring a large set of results. Going through a large result-set will mean more "clicks" and more cumbersome for the users. Now if you have a lot of attributes (than needed), that may be "overkill" as well!

The best way is to try it out and look at both the extremes. See what brings the best results for you. Having more attributes than needed is also not desired. There has to be a balance between the two approaches.

Generally the decision on attributes is driven by the searches that users need to perform, or the way the content "behaves" within the repository. By behavior, I mean if the file (or files) needs to be routed to other users, based on an attribute.

Similarly, you may want to change the lifecycle state of a file, based on a value of some attributes. Behavior of content means anything that happens to the file within a repository; whether it is routed; change of security; change of format; change of its status; archiving actions, or any automatic action that you want the system to take. More on this behavior is being covered in the business process management sections in later chapters.

Once you figure out the taxonomy and meta-data, you will automatically start thinking of the security/access. Each organization has its own requirements for the content security/access. Talking to a good content management consultant can help you figure out the best way to organize your content, attributes and security.

A word of caution on security: Security/access can be very granular and multi-dimensional; and it can go out of hands rather quickly, making it difficult to maintain. It reminds me of a particular client that had hundreds of thousands of files in their repository and the IT guys were assigning specific access to specific people on an individual files. Within few weeks of going live, merely keeping a track of who has what access of which files was a nightmare.

Keep it simple, stupid[4]

Keeping the security simple would eventually help you in the long run. This will also trigger discussions on grouping of users so that the security is based on user-groups, driven by attributes or driven by taxonomy. Taking a holistic approach and not worrying about specific files/folders would help you in the long run.

DISTRIBUTION OR PUBLISHING

By now, you would have known how to get your users access the content in repository. *How do you disperse (distribute) content to the relevant people?* I call it consumption of the content.

By consumption, I mean who all are supposed to look at the content. Apart from just consumption, the same (or other) users may

[4] *Source: Wikipedia*

need to "contribute" (to) the content as well. When you are looking at contribution, you can refer to the ingestion mechanisms described earlier, along with the security and access rights.

Most of the time, the mechanism (maybe a UI) you select for "contribution" or "consumption" (or *both*) would be based on the nature of your users and nature of your content.

Please remember that contribution is generally by internal users who are the authors of the content, or who edit the files in a repository. There are, however, many projects that I have dealt with where the contributions are done by people external to the organization. Take a look at your use-case (again).

Similarly, consumption can either be internal (maybe read-only users), or external. There may be a use-case where, based on the status (attribute) of a document, it may need to be routed to a print-stream for printing, or it may need to be published on a website, or be routed in an email. As I stated earlier, every project would be different. The key here is that apart from looking at how the content is added to the repository, you need to think of how it will be read (or *consumed*) by your users. This will also help you in some key licensing decisions.

Whenever you think of content being read (or consumed), you would need to look at the UI that will be sued by your users. I am sure your users would be interested in this aspect of the project.

Which UI is the best? Should I go with thick or thin client? Do I need to worry about controlling the printing? If so, how do I control the printing from the browser? Is it easy(ier) to customize the UI? Do I worry about generic viewers or allow the users to view the content using the individual applications? I have CAD or GIS content; do I need to worry about an integrated solution?

The simple answer is that there no ONE solution that will be the silver bullet for you. You would have to start breaking down all the use-cases and start selecting individual solutions to match those. A good business analyst can help you identify all the use-cases and an ECM consultant can start helping you put the appropriate solution against those use-cases. I have seen cases where an organization wants to standardize on the solutions, but fail to standardize on the use-cases. I would highly recommend going with a mixed approach to match your use-cases.

I recall years ago being a product manager of a generic viewer that was integrated with ECM systems and almost all of the projects had peculiar viewing use-cases (that the product did not handle well); despite the fact that ours was the first zero footprint solution with over 400 formats supported, *it was cutting-edge technology back then.*

For multi-media content, you can think of ways to stream the content. This helps in managing the response time to fetch the content from a repository. In fact, I have seen some document viewers also apply the same streaming concept to feed one page at a time so that the entire document (that may have thousands of pages) is not downloaded before displaying to the user. You can have one page at a time (on-demand viewing) in case of large files.

Similar to viewing, you can think of ways to control who all need to print the content. When dealing with browser-based systems, it would mean that one needs to control the printing controls of the browser. In thick-clients, this may be easy to do. In one of the projects, I saw that users were not allowed to access the content or take a screenshot or print. In the paper world, the users would make an appointment with the records staff and then go to the file-room and then look at whatever they needed to look at. In an ECM system we could control the access of who can edit and view the content, but it was cost prohibitive to control the printing or controlling the print-screen functions. The scope in that project did not permit us to customize the browser or the computer key-strokes. To address that, we implemented a kiosk model where users would still make the appointment and come to the records staff, but they would use computers there to access the pertinent content. The time it saved for staff to search and retrieve the content electronically was more than enough to justify the implementation.

Once you know how to distribute the content, you will find solutions that fit your use-case.

As part of content distribution strategy, you may have to route the content from the repository to a website. Many products have the features of managing the content on the web (termed as WCM, or Web Content Management). You can either go with one integrated solution where the content from within a repository gets published online and the publishing mechanism is all handled within one solution; or you can have an integrated solution where repository system hands over the content to be published to another system that does the publishing.

The best way that I have seen it work is if you segregate the publishing front-end from the back-end repository. That way, the front-end team responsible for maintaining and designing a portal (for wider audience) may just grab the content from the repository and take care of how to distribute the content. The business logic of publishing and un-publishing remains within the publishing engine, content remains in the repository and the front-end website (that displays the published content) is controlled by the respective designers. Having separate teams, specialized in their own functions would yield best results.

I would recommend having people take care of their own specialty. Just don't expect a back-end developer to create a portal and vice-versa. *Let them work on what they are good at.*

RETENTION/ARCHIVING

This should generally be a part of an ECM strategy, no matter if this is being implemented right away or is going to be a future endeavor. To address this, you would need to take a deeper look into records management, retention management and archiving. Talking to a consultant who has actually implemented a records management system would be very helpful.

Retention management, in simple terms means how we are going to retain the content in the repository. There might be policies that determine this. These policies can be corporate policies, legal regulations or industry standards. These policies are generally governed by the legal teams. As an implementation manager, your task would be to obtain a copy of the retention policies from the legal department. Many regulated environments also will have *file-plans* that dictate how to file the official records in the repository.

Whenever retention management is being implemented, try to address the following questions:

What the type of content needs to be retained; how long would it be retained (referred as retention period); what is the driving factor that starts this retention period; this driving factor can be an incident at a particular time (maybe value of an attribute gets changed, or user clicks something, or driven by some business logic if something happens, then start this retention period); what happens to the content after the retention period is over? What happens to the content during the retention period?

Talking of retention, an incident comes to my mind. One of the clients I worked with had their own perception about retention. This was pre-ECM implementation and this specific client had the content in a simple file-system.

The business users (and even the IT and legal) used to called the content under retention when the retention period was over. They had some files (contracts) that needed to be retained for 1 year after the execution-date. After one year, the users (and legal team) would send a communique that a specific file is now in retention. They all knew that it had something to do with retention and hence were calling the "disposition" as retention. It took me a while to change their perception 180 degree opposite.

Retention and Disposition are two separate concepts!

Now we know that retention strategy deals with something that triggers the content to be retained: this can be an event in time. This event may be driven by change in the behavior of content.

Think of it as if something has to tell the system that now let's retain this content and mark it in a way that the clock (retention clock) starts. Various ECM systems treat it differently, but try and look at the trigger(s) to start the retention clock. These can be as simple as a user clicks something in the system and the retention clock starts. Or it can be as complex as applying business logic to get the execution-date from an electronic signature, based on the status of the file, finds the linked files, update their attribute-values and then start the retention-clock on one of the linked-files.

Whatever the case is, one has to look for what determines the start of the retention clock. Since we are dealing with a point in time, it is a unit of time. This can be termed as a *base-date* of retention period.

Now that the clock started, what happens to the individual file? Generally, when the retention clock starts, that file would be marked as *"an official record under retention"* and users would typically be not able to delete or alter that content. Again, this is a general guideline and each situation/system may be different. The idea is that the content under retention needs to be marked by the system (for further disposition).

Now what happens to the content after the retention period is over?

Means at some point in time, the clock would tell the system that it is time to take the next action. The next action here can be termed as *"Disposition"*. Disposition strategy would tell the system what to do after the retention period. Disposition strategy is also owned by the legal teams and is part of retention policies. *A simple disposition may be "delete (electronically shred) the files completely".*

Disposition may dictate moving the content to an archival, long-term storage, or it may mean to save the attributes, but delete the content-files. And Disposition can be manual or automatic (depending on the system). Talk to the legal teams and understand retention policies and disposition fully before selecting a particular solution.

Now what happens if there are legal proceedings and you don't want to shred the content automatically? In those cases, there are options available in ECM systems to put the content under freeze (or holds). These will mean different things for different ECM systems. Just know that there are mechanisms in present-day systems to stop the clock from ticking because there might be some content that doesn't need to be deleted as per its retention policy.

Keeping the content in appropriate archival formats is also a key consideration. You can look at various formats (for example PDF-A and its variations) that may be available in the ECM products being implemented. The idea is to keep the content in archival formats, if the policy dictates to retain it for a long time.

Talk to the ECM consultants about tiered storage as that can be leveraged while planning the archival strategy.

I have seen that some organizations having one retention policy that says to keep the content indefinitely. But that defeats the purpose of having any retention management.

The purpose of retention management is to ensure that the appropriate content gets retained within a repository. The key word here is "appropriate". Whatever does not need to be retained should not be kept in the system.

* * *

BPM & Case Management

Going back to how the content behaves fits within the realm of BPM (or business process management): it is an inherent function of ECM systems these days.

The way document management is an important part of the content strategy, you have to consider the automation that one can bring if your content is well organized and centralized.

Typically BPM is in addition to the library services and may result in added costs. You have to compare the license costs as well as ease of maintenance of the business process automation.

Lot of times, the terms workflow and BPM are used to define automation.

Workflows are a set of rules that coordinate the interactions between people and systems. Think of workflows as routing mechanisms within a system.

BPM, however, is a more holistic approach to coordinate the work across *all* the available resources – people, information, machines, systems etc. A broader set of resources need a different approach for automation.

It would not be wrong to say that workflows are a subset of BPM mechanism; workflows can be one piece of puzzle in BPM automation. Whenever you are thinking of implementing a BPM system, consider the following:

- Process Definition
- Model Driven Environment
- Content Management
- Collaboration
- Workflow Automation
- Process/Rules Management, Analysis and Optimization
- Business Intelligence, Activity Monitoring, Reporting
- Enterprise Application Integration

Often times, I have seen organizations implementing a BPM system, without considering changing their existing process. Whatever works in a manual-world may not work exactly the same way in an electronic-world; it may not work at all.

Business Process Optimization (or at times Business Process Re-engineering – BPE) should always be part of a BPM implementation. If there is no optimization/reengineering, then what is the benefit of spending so much time and effort in getting a new platform implemented? You should always look for areas that can be automated, changed, and optimized whenever there is a BPM implementation going on.

Almost every major product out there has a way to simulate the processes. Consider that aspect when you are looking at the products. You want to know the gains that you would get from process automation without actually running the process in real-life. You should be able to simulate it and then get to know the metrics. Whenever you are talking with the vendors, ask about simulating the process and show the gains.

Apart from simulation, designing and maintaining the business process is also very important. Almost all the clients that I speak with, they want to maintain the processes after the initial implementation. The business-users know their process the best. You should rely on the business analyst to map the business process and then ask the ECM consultants to demonstrate how easy is to create and maintain the process in a BPM system.

We have now seen that the content can be organized into logical hierarchies, can be bound by attributes, and can be routed through a BPM mechanism for resources (people or systems) to take action. This bundled transaction of the content can be termed as *Case-Management.*

Case management is described as operating on bundles of content rather than individual documents or images.[5]

If you go back to our example of the HR repository where a package of HR documents is logically bound by folders and attributes. That entire package can be routed to users within an organization as a case. The case in that example would be employee's records, bound by employee ID.

Similarly, case management can be seen in insurance, appeals, public requests, taxes etc. Wherever there is a need to logically "bind" multiple documents (no matter where they exist in the repository); and route them as a business process, we can identify case management.

[5] *Source: AIIM*

BPM is now considered a critical component of operational intelligence to deliver real-time, actionable information. This information can be acted upon in a variety of ways; alerts to be sent to executives, dashboards, activity monitoring etc. Now that you have content, figured out a way to optimize the process, you should find ways to monitor the process.

Take a look at activity monitoring (either real-time or via reports) when you are implementing a BPM system (in conjunction with ECM). You need these data points for improving the business process going forward.

BPM systems can be pretty complex and the discussion can go beyond just content. I have discussed BPM in the context of ERP and the Application Integrations (EAI) separately.

We just need to ensure that we don't miss out on the BPM aspect of an ECM implementation; there are always opportunities to leverage Case Management in an ECM project.

* * *

Integrations

As Technology has evolved; there is always a need to share information from one system to another. We have seen almost all the systems "talking" to each other in an enterprise. In the context of *content*, you would see a need to integrate an ECM with other systems (be it ERP, legacy, line of business), no matter what!

There can be various ways how data gets exchanged from one system to another. Use of web-services is fairly common, as well as some organizations going with database driven integrations. It all depends on what type of information needs to be exchanged between the systems and if it needs to be in real-time or can wait. It also depends on if the systems have the required hooks (API) to allow this "communication". You should be able to integrate your ECM system with virtually any system out there. If web-service API is not available, then there would be database-level data exchange. Get the technical folks engaged in these discussions. You would, however, need to find out what information needs to be exchanged.

In case of dealing with legacy systems, I have seen the use of screen scraping technique. As per its traditional definition, the term "*screen scraping*" usually refers to a technique used to fetch screen data from one application and to be passed on to another.

It is sometimes confused with content scraping, which is the use of manual or automatic means to harvest content from either a website, or from a data-source. If there is a need of getting the input from a legacy system, take a look at the screen scraping options available.

Getting an ECM consultant who is aware of the options available would help you during the project. Knowing the options available and having those addressed would only mean that you don't get surprises later in the project. Looking at integration options available, would, not necessarily mean less moving parts, but would ensure that these parts move seamlessly.

* * *

Roll out and Adoption

THE IDENTIFIED SUCCESS CRITERIA that we discussed while planning a project is an important aspect of any project. This will dictate how well the users receive the system.

In fact this is single most important factor that determines if the system gets a positive publicity or is dumped down the line.

How well the users will take a change would depend on how well you have managed the change in your organization. *A change is a change, is a change.*

If you are implementing something totally

new (either from a UI perspective, or not), it becomes even more important to manage that change. You should certainly try and start planning for change management within your organization early-on in a project.

Whenever a new client asks me what is the biggest risk that will determine the success of a rollout, I always say *(well, almost always)* that it is the change management.

Whether you want to focus on more training, selection of the appropriate UI, how well you manage your requirements, how well the system gets designed, or how well the IT teams work ... All that depends on your project and on your organization. The key here is that one must not lose sight of this.

As discussed earlier, the selection of the UI is an important factor and you should go with specific UI for specific purposes. Having a complex UI only confuses users. Start nimble with fewer features at first, then think of ways to enhance the features later-on.

While selecting the products, you can try to find out how easy is customizing the UI so that your users are not overwhelmed by the options available. Going back to the earlier comment: *Keep it simple, stupid;* this principle has never failed me.

The mantra here would to *go-slow* when rolling out a large implementation.

Conclusion

TO CONCLUDE, I must state that this, by no means, is a full list of all the aspects of an ECM implementation. There are so many other factors that can affect the success of any project.

While implementing any project, you should certainly look for strong project management and consulting resources. While some project management can be provided by the internal teams, you need to ensure that team that is implementing the ECM project have seasoned resources who have done similar implementations in the past.

Whether you go with Agile, or water-fall implementation methodology, it is your prerogative.

The best project methodology is what works for the specific organization and the scenario.

Though, not guaranteeing success, I am sure if the factors given in this book are considered, it will just mean less surprises in the project. *Who needs surprises!*

* * *

About the Author

Aman Bhullar, with his 20 plus years of experience in the enterprise software industry tries to bridge the gap between the technology and the business. He is presently based in Southern California. Not a stranger to technology; he is always looking for innovative ways to help the organization manage their ECM and ERP initiatives. He can be contacted at:

amanbhullar@gmail.com.

Acknowledgments

Many thanks to all the people that I have worked with all these years; this memorable journey still continues. Every person I meet, every client I talk to, every engagement I take on, every project that I am part of, has provided an opportunity to learn.

Thanks for reading! Please share a short review and let me know what you thought!

You can either leave an online review on the website where you have purchased this book, or feel free to email me at amanbhullar@gmail.com.

Thanks and good luck!

Aman Bhullar